SUBHAS CHANDRA BOSE

AN INDOMITABLE SPIRIT OF THE INDIAN FREEDOM MOVEMENT

Manasvi Vohra

Published by:

V&S PUBLISHERS

F-2/16, Ansari Road, Daryaganj, New Delhi - 110002
☎ 23240026, 23240027 • *Fax:* 011-23240028
✉ info@vspublishers.com • 🌐 www.vspublishers.com

 **Online Brand Store: amazon.in/vspublishers**

Regional Office: Hyderabad

5-1-707/1, Brij Bhawan (Beside Central Bank of India Lane)
Bank Street, Koti, Hyderabad - 500 095
☎ 040-24737290
✉ vspublishershyd@gmail.com

Follow us on:   

BUY OUR BOOKS FROM: AMAZON FLIPKART

© Copyright: *V&S* PUBLISHERS
ISBN 978-81-978303-8-9
New Edition

DISCLAIMER

While every attempt has been made to provide accurate and timely information in this book, neither the author nor the publisher assumes any responsibility for errors, unintended omissions or commissions detected therein. The author and publisher make no representation or warranty with respect to the comprehensiveness or completeness of the contents provided.

All matters included have been simplified under professional guidance for general information only without any warranty for applicability on an individual. Any mention of an organization or a website in the book by way of citation or as a source of additional information doesn't imply the endorsement of the content either by the author or the publisher. It is possible that websites cited may have changed or removed between the time of editing and publishing the book.

Results from using the expert opinion in this book will be totally dependent on individual circumstances and factors beyond the control of the author and the publisher.

It makes sense to elicit advice from well informed sources before implementing the ideas given in the book. The reader assumes full responsibility for the consequences arising out from reading this book.

For proper guidance, it is advisable to read the book under the watchful eyes of parents/guardian. The purchaser of this book assumes all responsibility for the use of given materials and information.

The copyright of the entire content of this book rests with the author/publisher. Any infringement/ transmission of the cover design, text or illustrations, in any form, by any means, by any entity will invite legal action and be responsible for consequences thereon.

Publisher's Note

Since the beginning of our operations in 2010, **V&S Publishers** has been devoted to bringing you one of the best and widest selections of books from across reading genres. Our work is defined by our very name, Value and Substance (V&S), which is at the heart of the books we publish. In becoming one of the leading publishers of general trade books in the mass-appeal genre in India, we have focused on developing a repertoire of titles that not just seek to inspire our readers to grow and flourish in life, but also spark a love for varied cultures and languages. Today, our catalogue has expanded to more than 1000 titles, across the categories of academic, children's stories, parenting, popular science, religion and spirituality, self-improvement, and many more.

Subhas Chandra Bose, Netaji, is one of India's most influential freedom fighters whose determination and commitment to the cause of independence has left an indelible mark on the nation's history. This biography meticulously chronicles the life of a person who became a symbol of courage, strength and patriotism.

His journey from an extraordinary student to a revolutionary leader is a testimony to his indomitable spirit and strategic acumen. Bose believed in complete independence and struggled for it uncompromisingly. Bose's leadership and famous call to his countrymen, "Give me blood, and I will give you freedom," ignited flames of patriotism among the Indians and motivated them to join the freedom struggle. This biography delves deep into the complexities of Bose's life, his ideological differences with contemporaries like Gandhi and his mysterious disappearance. Bose's vision and legacy continues to inspire new generations.

We sincerely hope our effort in bringing out this offering will be greeted by the warm and enthusiastic reception of our readers.

Contents

1

Childhood and Early Life

Subhas Chandra Bose was born during the 19th century, in Calcutta. This period was marked by influential movements and political unrest, leaving a lasting impact on Indian society.

Subhas Chandra Bose was born into a privileged Bengali family on 23rd January 1897, in Cuttack. Cuttack was a part of the Bengal Province in British India, specifically the Orissa Division. Subhas had a close bond with his mother, Prabhavati Bose, who greatly influenced their family life. At the young age of 14, Prabhavati Devi had given birth to the first of her 14 children. Subhas was the ninth child among his siblings.

Subhas's father, Jankinath Bose, was a renowned lawyer, who exhibited legal diligence in legal matters, throughout his life. He was a loyal supporter of the British Imperial government. Bose exhibited diligence in legal matters throughout his life.

(a) Prabhavati Bose, mother of Subhas Chandra Bose

(b) Jankinath Bose, father of Subhas Chandra Bose

(c) Subhas Chandra Bose with his brother Sarat Chandra Bose

Early years

Subhas Chandra Bose came from a Bengali family that relocated to different parts of northern India due to the high demand for professionals like lawyers, doctors, judges, and clerks. This demand stemmed from the fact that English-educated Bengalis in Calcutta held most of the government positions and liberal occupations. The Boses originally came from neighbouring villages near Calcutta, such as Kodalia, Harinavi, and Rajpur.

A Diligent Student
Subhas Chandra Bose was an outstanding student. Throughout his school and university studies, he received top grades. In 1918, he graduated with honours in Philosophy.

From an early age, Subhas shared a strong bond with his mother, who instilled deep love for the country in him. Even as a young boy of 12, he wrote heartfelt letters to his mother, showing immense respect for her. Even later, when he was involved in the fight for India's independence, he never forgot his mother and often spoke of how much he owed to her. Unlike many political and social reformers, who distanced themselves from their families, Subhas Chandra Bose held his mother and other family members in high regard. This was largely due to the close-knit nature of the Bose family, with Prabhavati and Jankinath Bose at its core.

Jankinath was not only a renowned lawyer but also a respected social reformer. He believed that his children needed an English education to succeed in the future. Consequently, in January 1902, Subhas, along with his five older brothers, was enrolled in the Baptist Mission's Protestant European School in Cuttack.

The school primarily had students of European or Anglo-Indian background, and English served as the primary medium of instruction. The curriculum included subjects like Latin, the

Bible, British history, Geography, and lessons on manners. No Indian vernacular languages were taught. This differed from the Bose household, where only Bengali was spoken. Subhas's mother, a devout Hindu, regularly worshiped Hindu goddesses like Durga and Kali. She not only sang devotional songs but also shared stories from *Ramayana* and *Mahabharata* with her children.

While Jankinath was often occupied with his professional commitments, Prabhavati played a vital role in Subhas's upbringing. Subash's father's love for English literature influenced many of his sons, but it was Subash's mother, who nurtured his compassionate spirit, inspiring him to help those in need.

Striking a balancing act

In 1909, at the age of 12, Subhas began attending Ravenshaw Collegiate School in Cuttack, along with his his five brothers. At this school, Subash learned Bengali, Sanskrit, and the Hindu scriptures like the Vedas and Upanishads. While he continued with his Western education, he started to wear Indian clothing and pondered over matters of religion. In a letter to his mother, he mentioned his familiarity with the ideas of Ramakrishna Paramahamsa and Swami Vivekananda.

Ravenshaw Collegiate School was attended by Subhas Chandra Bose

During this time, young Subhas grappled with the conflict between the Indian and Western ways of life. Despite his father's emphasis on the importance of an English education, Subhas could not disregard the influence of his mother and his teacher, Beni Madhav Das, at Ravenshaw, who instilled in him a love for nature. By the age of 14, he seemed to have resolved this cultural conflict, as evident from a letter to his mother where he acknowledged the significance of honouring the traditions followed by his forefathers.

Despite his internal struggle over culture and lifestyle, Subhas was an intelligent student. In his matriculation exam in 1912, he achieved the second position.

Years in Presidency College

By 1913, Subhas Chandra Bose was attending Presidency College, located in Calcutta, as was the tradition then for the upper-caste Hindu men of Bengal. Here, he studied philosophy, which included the thoughts of Kant, Bergson, and Hegel, among others. Subhas felt out of place in college. This was because unlike other students, who also came from wealthy backgrounds and aspired to pass their exams to find good government jobs, Subhas was more spiritual, with well-developed socio-political beliefs.

Main Gate of college attended by Subhas Chandra Bose, Calcutta

A Slogan for a Lifetime
Subhas Chandra Bose developed "Jai Hind," one of India's most iconic phrases. He also chose Rabindranath Tagore's *Jana Gana Mana* as his favoured national anthem.

Soon, he befriended Hemanta Kumar Sarkar, who became his partner in exploring religious ideas. In 1914, during vacation, they both embarked on an adventure to northern India to find a spiritual guru to guide them. However, Subhas's family did clearly know about this trip. They thought he had run away. Unfortunately, young Subhas fell sick with typhoid during the trip and subsequently returned home. In the months to follow, Subhas returned to

Hemanta Kumar Sarkar

Presidency College to pursue his studies. What followed was a series of events that sealed his fate as a national hero in the years to come.

2

Cambridge and Indian National Congress

On 15th September 1919, a young Subhas embarked on his journey to Cambridge, United Kingdom, just a few weeks before the Armistice Agreement marked the end of World War I. At this time, the Jallianwala Bagh Massacre had already occurred, yet the full extent of the tragedy remained unknown to the people of India. Meanwhile, Mahatma Gandhi, emerged as a prominent leader in India's independence movement, who travelled the country to gauge the public's response to this tragedy.

In England, young Subhas was not deeply affected by the events of the massacre for two reasons. Firstly, he was immersed in his studies, diligently preparing for the Indian Civil Services (ICS) examination. Secondly, the British press of the time presented a convoluted account of the Jallianwala Bagh massacre, leaving Indians in England unable to fully grasp the gravity of the situation.

Subhas Chandra Bose in Cambridge in 1919

Enrolling at Cambridge University

On 20th October, 1919 Subhas began the application process for the ICS. He listed Lord Sinha of Raipur, Under Secretary of State for India, and Bhupendranath Basu, a prosperous Calcutta lawyer who served on the Council of India in London, as his references. He also sought admission to a college within the University of Cambridge and sought assistance from Indian students and the Non-Collegiate Students Board.

Subhas officially enrolled at the University on 19th November, 1919. Simultaneously, he commenced his preparations for the ICS examination. However, he soon realised that the subjects he had chosen were quite challenging: Philosophy, Political Science, English History, European History, Geography, Economics, Law, English Composition, and Sanskrit. These subjects had not been extensively covered during his schooling in India. Consequently, he made the decision to dedicate all his time to studying and mastering these subjects.

Resigning from Civil Services
In 1919, Subhas Chandra Bose finished fourth in the coveted Indian Civil Services Exam. He later resigned from this position.

In August 1920, young Subhas undertook the ICS examination and remarkably secured the fourth rank among all the candidates that year. However, he now faced a profound dilemma – whether to accept a position within the British Government or not.

To unravel this quandary, Subhas penned a heartfelt letter to the renowned Bengali leader and lawyer, C.R. Das, laying bare his personal and spiritual struggles. He earnestly sought guidance on how best to serve India. Deep down, he had already made the firm resolve to forego a career in the Indian Civil Service and instead commit his life to the service of his nation. C.R. Das, in response, wholeheartedly encouraged him to return to India.

Subhas also corresponded with his father and his brother, Sarat Chandra Bose. In one of his letters to Sarat, he candidly described his inner turmoil in the following manner:

"But for a man of my temperament who has been feeding on ideas that might be called eccentric—the line of least resistance is not the best line to follow ... The uncertainties of life are not appalling to one who has not, at heart, worldly ambitions. Moreover, it is not possible to serve one's country in the best and fullest manner if one is chained on to the civil service."

By April 1921, Subhas had firmly decided not to pursue the ICS examination. He promptly wrote to Sarat, conveying his choice and offering apologies for the distress it might cause his mother, father, and other family members. Subhas completed his Cambridge B.A. Final Examinations with a somewhat lacklustre effort. Although he managed to pass, his grades placed him in the Third Division. In June, he began preparations for his return to India.

This phase in Subhas's life served as a prelude to the numerous innovative endeavours he would undertake later on. It established the foundation for situations he would encounter in the future, where he would focus on problem-solving and the decisiveness of his choices.

Joining the Indian National Congress

After resigning from the Indian Civil Service, Bose was resolute in his commitment to serve India. At the age of 24, he arrived in Bombay on 16th July

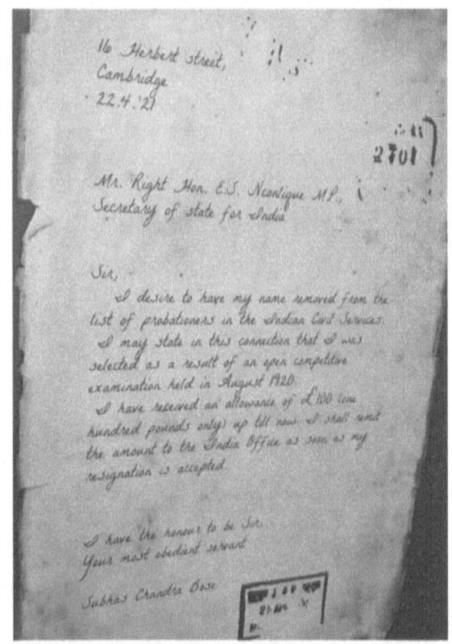

Original resignation letter written by Subhas Chandra Bose for resigning from the ICS

1921, nearly a year and a half after the Indian National Congress (INC) had already conducted the Nagpur session, during which the party had adopted Gandhi's principle of non-violent non-cooperation with the British Government.

Subhas Chandra Bose sharing a moment with Mahatama Gandhi

Upon his arrival in Bombay, Bose headed straight to Mahatma Gandhi's residence on Laburnum Road. There, he engaged in a significant and lengthy conversation with the 51-year-old Gandhi regarding the initiatives he had taken for the freedom movement. Bose posed questions about these programs, seeking clarity on how to best serve his country. However, Gandhi's responses did not satisfy Bose nor did they provide a definitive solution to his dilemma.

President of All India National Congress

Subhas Chandra Bose served as the President of the All India National Congress on two separate occasions.

This divergence arose from the differing approaches of Gandhi and Bose towards freedom struggle. While Gandhi advocated non-violent means to achieve objectives like Satyagraha and Swaraj, Bose believed that all methods whether violent or non-violent were acceptable in the quest for freedom from British rule. They also held contrasting views on the ultimate goals of governance, with Bose being drawn to the totalitarian model, a perspective Gandhi wholly rejected.

After arriving in Calcutta, Bose arranged a meeting with C.R. Das, leading to a series of conversations where he sought to comprehend the INC's objectives. In contrast to Gandhi, Das was sympathetic to the ideals of young, idealistic men like Bose, who endorsed extremism. Das played a pivotal role in propelling Bose into nationalist politics, providing him with a clear path forward: dedicating himself to the movement initiated by Gandhi. Subsequently, Bose worked with the INC for approximately 20 years.

Bose published a newspaper called **"Swaraj"** and assumed responsibility for the publicity of the Bengal Provincial Committee. In 1923, he was elected as the President of the India Youth Congress and became the Secretary of the Bengal State Congress. When Das became the Mayor of Calcutta in 1924, Bose took on the role of CEO of the Calcutta Municipal Corporation. During this period, he gained a reputation for being a capable administrator and for instituting numerous changes in the city's administration.

Subhas Chandra Bose greeted by municipal corporation officials, in Calcutta in 1930

Unfortunately, in 1925, C.R. Das passed away, leaving Bose without a mentor. Subash was relatively young and felt adrift. His correspondence with Das's wife, Basanti Devi, reflected his state of mind during this period. Bose was disheartened and felt lost without the guidance of a mentor like C.R. Das. In the same year, he led a protest march in Calcutta, but he was arrested and imprisoned along with other leaders. Subsequently, he was transferred to Mandalay Jail in Burma (now Myanmar), where he contracted tuberculosis. He remained incarcerated there for two years and was released in May 1927 due to his deteriorating health.

□□□

3

Travels in Europe and Differences with the INC

After his release from Mandalay Jail in 1927, Bose spent some time in solitude to cope with the loss of C.R. Das. Soon afterward, he assumed the role of President of the Bengal Provincial Congress Committee and resumed his political activities. During this period, India was in turmoil due to the British Government's establishment of the Simon Commission. The British had set up this commission to review constitutional reforms in India. The lack of Indian representation led to protests, fuelling demands for self-rule.

Bose actively engaged in the agitation against the Simon Commission and played a prominent role in the youth movement across the nation. He later got elected as the President of the All India Youth Congress, an event that took place in Calcutta in 1928. Additionally, he became the General Officer Commanding of the Volunteer Corps, responsible for maintaining order during Congress meetings. In the same year, Bose joined forces with Jawaharlal Nehru to establish a Left-wing faction within the Congress, advocating for radical measures against the government.

Subhas Chandra Bose with Jawaharlal Nehru

Following the Calcutta Congress, Bose assumed the presidency of the All India Trade Union Congress, a position he held until 1931. This marked a significant turning point for Bose, as he had successfully developed his own image and identity since C.R. Das's passing. This role instilled in him the confidence that he could lead independently without relying on guidance from others.

His leadership as the President of the All India Trade Union Congress garnered popularity among leftists in the country and allowed him to align the working classes with the freedom movement. By 1930, Bose had emerged as one of the most prominent figures within the Congress party, following the stature of Mahatma Gandhi and Jawaharlal Nehru.

Bose's travels to Europe

In 1932, Bose travelled to Vienna due to suspected tuberculosis. During his time there, he had meetings with the renowned Indian leader and former President of Indian Legislative Assembly,

Vithalbhai Patel. In these discussions, both Patel and Bose reached a shared belief that India couldn't attain independence without the support from foreign nations. Both of them viewed the development of international connections as crucial for integrating the Indian Nationalist Movement into global affairs. This strategy aimed to apply pressure on Britain, compelling it to grant India immediate independence.

> **A Legacy of Support**
>
> Vithalbhai Patel left his wealth in a will to Subhas Chandra Bose to support the anti-British campaign abroad. This highlighted a shared vision among the two Congress leaders for expanding the Indian National Congress's activities beyond India's borders. However, this bequest led to legal disputes in the Bombay High Court.

Mahatma Gandhi believed that India would grab the world's attention if Indians obstructed the British Government's operations within the country. He thought this would force the world to take notice. While Congress adhered to this idea for years, Patel and Bose disagreed. The reason behind such disagreement was that, the people outside India did not know how the British treated Indians, with all news outlets under British control. This international ignorance about India's situation and the suffering of its people allowed the British to avoid discussing Indian independence.

In 1934, Bose returned to India without the Government's permission to visit his ailing father, who eventually passed away. He soon returned to Europe and stayed there until 1936. During his stay in Europe, Bose engaged with Indian students and European politicians, including the Italian leader Benito Mussolini. Bose also participated in a conference organised by Indian students in Vienna and addressed a gathering at the Asiatic Students' Conference in Rome. He closely observed party organisation, communism, and fascism in daily life.

He also visited Ireland, meeting De Valera and establishing connections with various European political figures.

During this time, he dedicated himself to research and wrote his book, *The Indian Struggle*, which covered the Indian independence movement from 1920 to 1934. The book was published in London in 1935 but was subsequently banned by the British Government due to concerns that it might spark protests.

<table>
<tr><td>

Finding Love

In 1934, Bose was introduced to Emilie Schenkl by a mutual friend. Emilie had excellent skills in shorthand, English, and typing. They fell in love and secretly married in a Hindu ceremony on 26th December 1937, in Bad Gastein.
</td></tr>
</table>

Subhas Chandra Bose with Emilie Schenkl in 1937

Differences within the Indian National Congress

In February 1938, Bose returned to India and presided over a Congress session, which went on to be a landmark moment in India's independence movement. He initiated the National

Planning Committee, with Pandit Jawaharlal Nehru as its first Chairman, and he took on the role of Convener.

As Bose's presidency neared its end, he sought re-election for a longer tenure. Gandhi disapproved and nominated Dr. Pattabhi Sitaramayya, leading to strong disagreements and the resignation of most of the Congress Working Committee. Bose proceeded with his candidacy, leading to a rift among the members and the formation of Left and Right-wing factions within the party.

Subhash Chandra Bose addressing
Congress session in 1938 among other freedom fighters

Netaji's Unique Tribute to Gandhi

Subhas Chandra Bose referred to Mahatma Gandhi as the "Patriot of Patriots," despite their differing political ideologies, displaying remarkable magnanimity.

During this time, Bose fell ill, rendering him unable to actively participate in the open session of Congress and the Working Committee meetings. At the Tripuri session, he pushed for an ultimatum to the British, demanding independence within six months, failing which India would begin a mass-scale freedom struggle. However, Gandhi opposed this proposal, leading to its subsequent abandonment by Congress. Despite his illness, Bose remained convinced that war in Europe was imminent and insisted on issuing a final warning to the British.

Neta Ji addressing National Planning Committee (NPC) on December 17, 1938

As all efforts to resolve the dispute between the left and right wings of the Congress failed, Bose resigned from the presidency. On 22nd June 1939, he founded the All India Forward Bloc within the Congress, seeking support from the political left across India. However, its primary backing came from his home state of Bengal. U Muthuramalingam Thevar, who had long been an ardent supporter of Bose also joined the Forward Bloc.

In September 1939, as Bose had foreseen, Europe was embroiled in war. Under the leadership of Bose, the Forward Bloc initiated an anti-British propaganda campaign. Bose organised a massive civil disobedience movement to protest Viceroy Lord Linlithgow's unilateral decision to involve India in the war without consulting Congress leaders. He also demanded the removal of the Holwell Monument in Dalhousie Square, which commemorated those who perished in the Black Hole (a dungeon at Fort William) of Calcutta.

As the Forward Bloc gained strength as a formidable opposition force, Bose and his colleagues faced arrest in July 1940. When the British Government refused to put him on trial, he issued an ultimatum, threatening an indefinite hunger strike unless he was released.

Bose after release from prison with
Prabhavati Bose, Satish Chandra Bose and Abdur Rahman Siddiqi, 1940

An Iconic Freedom Fighter

Subhas Chandra Bose faced imprisonment 11 times between 1921 and 1941. He served as the Mayor of Calcutta in 1930 while he was still in prison.

Initially, the British Government dismissed his ultimatum, but they soon recognised the growing support for him and the sensitivity of the situation. They quietly released him but placed him under house arrest. In a surprising turn of events, after 40 days of internment, Bose reportedly vanished from his Calcutta home, leaving no trace. In April 1942, he resurfaced as the head of Azad Hind Radio in Berlin, marking a new chapter in the Indian freedom struggle.

4

Bose in Nazi Germany

So, how did Bose escape to Nazi Germany, and why did he choose this path? To answer these questions, we must delve into Bose's core ideology. From the very start of his association with the Congress, Bose harboured doubts about the practicality of Gandhi's principles of non-violence, non-cooperation, and *satyagraha* as effective tools for gaining independence from British rule. He initially joined the Congress at the urging of C.R. Das, despite his reservations. However, as the movement gained momentum and widespread participation in India, Bose and some of his colleagues began reconsidering their stance.

The rapid evolution of the movement provided young revolutionaries like Bose with confidence. They believed that if the movement could become truly revolutionary, it would create a political crisis that could force the British out of the country. After all, Gandhi had successfully connected the elitist leaders of the freedom movement with the masses.

During this period, it is notable that the elite enjoyed a standard of living and education up to 20 times higher than that of the masses. In this context, Bose recognised that Gandhi, with his profound understanding of rural India, Gandhi had the ability to unite the Indian population for a common cause. Bose and his associates could not accomplish this on their own due to their limited knowledge of village conditions and lack of contact with rural people.

Despite these factors, Bose persevered with his vision of orchestrating a revolutionary struggle to oust the British from India. He saw British rule as a military occupation that could only be countered through a large-scale revolution. His dilemma revolved around seeking assistance from Nazi Germany, despite Germany's imperialistic outlook, which had not inspired hope in the international arena.

Although Bose attempted to establish contact with a National Socialist and engage with German officials in the Foreign Office during his European sojourn, his efforts were in vain. Consequently, in 1941, Bose penned a letter to Dr. Thierfelder, the President of the Deutsche Akademie, a German cultural institution. In this letter, he denounced Hitler's derogatory remarks about Indians.

With the outbreak of World War II, Bose deduced that the conflict would weaken Britain's military and bolster the Indian movement against British rule. Thus, Bose's interest was not in National Socialist Germany per se; he was motivated by the belief that the war between Britain and Germany would benefit the oppressed nations.

Fleeing to Nazi Germany

Subhas Chandra Bose escaped his Calcutta residence in January 1941. Till today, this escape has been a subject of intrigue and controversy. While under house arrest by British authorities, Bose managed to elude his captors and made his getaway. The precise details of his escape remain shrouded in uncertainty, with various theories and accounts in circulation.

According to one narrative, a few days prior to his escape, Bose requested solitude and peace. This was merely a ruse to avoid the British guards, as he concealed his identity by growing a beard in hiding. On the night of 16th January 1941, he assumed the guise of a *Pathan*, donning brown overcoat and loose-fitting trousers. It is believed that he was accompanied by his nephew, Sisir Kumar Bose, on the night of his escape. Together, they purportedly reached Gomoh Railway Station (now known as Netaji Subhas Chandra Bose Gomoh Station) in Bihar (now Jharkhand).

Bose in House arrest and growing long beard to escape the arrest

According to this account, Bose is said to have reached Peshawar with the assistance of the Abwehr, a German military intelligence organisation during World War II. Upon his arrival in Peshawar, he found refuge in the home of Abad Khan, a friend of Akbar Shah, a prominent supporter of Bose's cause. Akbar Shah, a leader of the Forward Bloc, joined forces with Mohammed Shah and Bhagat Ram Talwar to aid Bose in his escape from British custody. These individuals shared a deep sympathy for India's independence struggle and actively supported Bose's efforts by seeking assistance from various sources.

By 26th January 1941, Bose was en route to Russia, travelling through the North-West Frontier in British India and Afghanistan. Akbar Shah was also on his way to the Soviet Union. Given Bose's inability to speak Pashto, which could have exposed him to Pashto-speaking individuals working for the British, Shah advised him to feign deafness and muteness and adopt the appearance of a tribesman by growing a long beard.

Bose received valuable assistance from the supporters of Aga Khan III to facilitate his journey to Afghanistan. During this phase, he encountered an Abwehr unit disguised as a team of road construction engineers associated with the Organisation Todt, a civil and military engineering group in Nazi Germany. With their assistance, Bose successfully crossed from Afghanistan through Kabul to reach the Soviet Union.

Meeting the Italian Foreign Minister
Netaji met the Italian Foreign Minister Galeazzo Ciano in 1941 to discuss the draft declaration of independence. He stayed in Rome with his wife for approximately six weeks.

Italian Foreign Minister Galeazzo Ciano in 1936

Upon his arrival in Russia, Bose was taken to Moscow by the NKVD, the primary security and secret police organisation in the Soviet Union during Joseph Stalin's rule. He held hopes that the strained relations between the British and Russia would garner Soviet support for his plans to incite a popular uprising in India. Unfortunately, their response fell short of his expectations.

Subsequently, Bose was transported to Moscow's German Ambassador, Count von der Schulenburg. In April, he was flown aboard a special courier aircraft to meet Joachim von Ribbentrop and officials from the German Foreign Ministry at the Wilhelmstrasse.

Arriving in Nazi Germany

Bose's involvement with the German Government during World War II had a strictly formal and purpose-driven nature. He never held admiration for Hitler or National Socialism in Germany. Notably, his collaborator in Berlin, Baron von Trott zu Solz, actively conspired to assassinate Hitler and overthrow his regime in July 1944, alongside Count Stauffenberg and others.

Upon his arrival in Germany, Bose was placed under the supervision of Baron von Trott, who headed the Special Bureau for India. This bureau was responsible for operating Azad Hind Radio, a German-sponsored broadcasting initiative. Baron von Trott became a close friend and mentor to Bose during his time in Berlin.

Timeless Slogans

Azad Hind Radio was established by Bose in Nazi Germany. He is also credited with coining noteworthy phrases, such as "Jai Hind," "Dilli chalo," and "Give me blood and I shall give you freedom."

Flag of the Azad Hind Legion

During his stay in Germany, Bose established the Free India Centre, which aimed to advance India's independence movement and secure support from Axis powers. The centre served as a focal point for Bose's activities and his efforts to solicit aid for India's struggle for freedom. Additionally, Bose also formed the Azad Hind Legion, which comprised Indian prisoners of war who had previously fought for the British in North Africa before being captured by Axis forces.

Bose was open to the idea of a Nazi troop invasion of India through the USSR, with the Azad Hind Legion taking the lead. However, this decision has been questioned by many, as it seemed unlikely that the Germans would voluntarily withdraw following such an invasion. Moreover, this scenario could have resulted in an Axis victory in the war.

5

Travels to Southeast Asia

Bose's time in Germany has often been a subject of criticism in India, primarily questioning the moral implications of initiating a movement abroad, especially in collaboration with fascist states. This criticism stems from a lack of awareness regarding Bose's involvement with the German resistance against Hitler. Additionally, many accounts of Bose's life do not delve into his disassociation from the Nazis in Germany. It is crucial to understand that he turned to Germany for assistance only because the USSR had refused to support him due to their alliance with Britain during World War II.

Examining excerpts from Bose's letters, writings, speeches, and statements reveals his clear opposition to Fascist ideologies. His upbringing, influenced by the ideas of Rabindranath Tagore, Swami Vivekananda, Sri Aurobindo, and Mahatma Gandhi, shaped him as a humanist with a commitment to inclusivity and liberalism. In one of his letters to Dr. Thierfelder, Bose explicitly states:

> *"...When we are fighting greatest Empire in the world for our freedom and for our rights and when we are confident of our ultimate success, we cannot brook any insult from any other nation or any attack on our race or culture."*

Bose held a strong commitment to the principles of racial equality and the freedom of all Asian and European nations. He vehemently opposed notions of racial superiority and extreme nationalism. Bose and Azad Hind Radio never endorsed the National Socialist Party in Europe or anywhere else globally. Amidst the backdrop of nationalism and fascism, he concentrated on using the political dynamics in the Western world to benefit India.

Establishing a Presence in Nazi Germany

In Nazi Germany, most of the Special Bureau for India's staff were assigned to assist Bose in the country. Historian Romain Hayes notes that the German Foreign Office arranged an opulent residence for Bose, complete with a cook, gardener, butler, and a chauffeured car. It was during this period that his wife, Emilie Schenkl, joined him in this residence. However, some, including Adam von Trott and a few of his associates, harboured suspicions about her presence, believing she sought a comfortable life during wartime (as mentioned by historian Leonard A. Gordon). In November 1942, the couple welcomed their daughter, Anita Bose.

Anita Bose, daughter of Subhas Chandra Bose

Initially, the Germans hesitated to form an alliance with Bose because he lacked the popularity of figures like Mahatma Gandhi and Jawaharlal Nehru. However, global dynamics were evolving rapidly. By 1942, Nazi Germany was facing defeat in the war and was deeply involved in the conflict with the USSR. Notably, nearly 3,000 Indian prisoners of war had joined the Azad Hind Fauj. While this achievement was significant, Bose remained concerned about the changing landscape. His keen intellect had already discerned that Germany would be unable to provide substantial assistance to India in its struggle against the British.

Bose's suspicions deepened during his meeting with Hitler in 1942. He came to the conclusion that Hitler primarily saw his men as tools for winning propaganda battles. Faced with this realization, Bose had to swiftly adapt his plans to the rapidly changing circumstances. Leaving the Azad Hind Fauj in Berlin was not an easy decision for him. During an emotional farewell, Bose expressed his regret that he had been unable to provide his brave soldiers with anything but hardship. He lamented his inability to give them presents or rewards for their valor, given their presence in a foreign land. This sense of dependence on foreigners for resources and his inability to finance the INA left him deeply frustrated.

Managing Finances

Subhas Chandra Bose was meticulous in financial matters. He was uncomfortable with foreign financing of his work. To rectify this, he raised money from Indians in East Asia and promptly repaid the loan from the Germans, as documented by the German Foreign Office. Bose was determined not to be indebted to any country in financial matters.

When Bose didn't receive the response he sought from Nazi Germany, he made the decision to relocate to Southeast Asia. Japan had achieved some victories by this point. Therefore, in February 1943, Bose embarked on a journey to Japan, leaving his wife and infant daughter behind. His travel plan involved initially boarding a German submarine and then transferring to a Japanese submarine to reach Southeast Asia.

Voyage to Southeast Asia

On February 8, 1943, Bose embarked on a remarkable sea voyage. He boarded the German submarine U-180, which sailed around the Cape of Good Hope and east of Madagascar. From there, he boarded the I-29, a Japanese submarine that would take him to Imperial Japan. This journey made history because it was the only civilian transfer between submarines from different navies during World War II.

But what motivated Bose to undertake this sea voyage to East Asia? Two primary reasons guided his decision. First, he desired proximity to India and the Indian community in Southeast Asia. He had learned that Indians in Southeast Asian countries were eager to support his campaign against British rule in India. Bose aimed to be among his fellow countrymen and reduce his reliance on foreign material support.

Upon reaching Southeast Asia, Subhas Chandra Bose's journey took a pivotal turn as he began laying the groundwork for a formidable force that would play a significant role in India's struggle for independence – the Indian National Army (INA). The INA was formed under the leadership of Subash Chandra Bose, comprising Indian prisoners of war liberated from British captivity and Indians residing in Southeast Asian countries who willingly offered themselves to serve

Uniform of Subhas Chandra Bose which he wore when he organized INA

the nation's purpose. The Indian National Army (INA) or Azad Hind Fauj was the larger force that Bose led, which included not only the Free India Legion but also other units and supporters from Southeast Asia. So, while the Free India Legion was established in Germany, it was part of Bose's broader efforts to build an army for India's liberation.

The Indian National Army was conceived by Japanese Major Iwaichi Fujiwara in World War II, with a mission to fight alongside the Japanese army. The INA's formation began when British Indian army captain Mohan Singh, recruited by Fujiwara, started discussions in December 1941. The name "Indian National Army" was agreed upon by Fujiwara and Singh in January 1942. Initially associated with the Indian Independence League in Tokyo, the first INA was disbanded in December 1942 due to disputes between the Hikari Kikan and Mohan Singh, who believed the Japanese High Command was exploiting them for propaganda.

The INA also had a unique women's unit, the Rani of Jhansi Regiment, led by Captain Lakshmi Swaminathan, a pioneering initiative in Asia.

Bose with the Rani Jhansi Regiment of INA

However, the idea was revived when Bose arrived in the Far East in 1943. In July, Rash Behari Bose handed over control of the organisation to Subhas Chandra Bose. He reorganised the fledgling army and gained massive support from the expatriate Indian community in Southeast Asia. They joined the INA and offered financial support for the cause of independence.

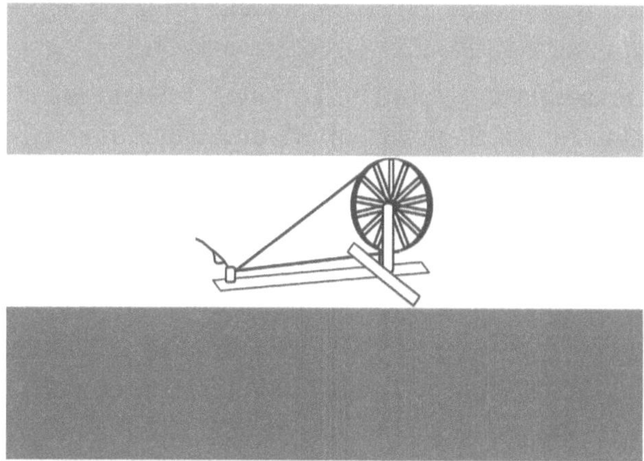

The flag on Indian National Army

Bose and INA

The INA's initial mission was to assist the Japanese advance in Eastern India, particularly in Manipur. They included special forces like the Bahadur Group, conducting operations behind enemy lines during diversions in Arakan and the Japanese offensive toward Imphal and Kohima.

Despite facing military setbacks, Bose maintained support for the Azad Hind movement. The INA operated under the Azad Hind Government, which established its own currency, stamps, legal system, and received recognition from nine Axis states, including Germany, Japan, and Italy. This government was involved in the Greater East Asia Conference in November 1943 as an observer.

In 1942, the Japanese took control of the Andaman and Nicobar Islands. A year later, the Provisional Government and INA were established there, with Lt Col. A.D. Loganathan as Governor General. The islands were renamed Shaheed (Martyr) and Swaraj (Independence), but the Japanese Navy retained control. During Bose's visit in early 1944, he was isolated from the locals, unaware of the Japanese administration's torture of Diwan Singh, a leader of the Indian Independence League who later died in Cellular Jail. Loganathan resigned as Governor General, realising his lack of genuine authority.

In the mainland, the Indian Tricolour, resembling the Indian National Congress flag, was raised for the first time in Moirang, Manipur. Kohima and Imphal were encircled and besieged by Japanese forces, the Burmese National Army, and INA brigades: the Gandhi and Nehru Brigades.

On July 6, 1944, Subhas Chandra Bose, speaking on Azad Hind Radio in Singapore, addressed Mahatma Gandhi as the "Father of the Nation" and sought his blessings for the ongoing war. This marked the first use of the term "Father of the Nation" for Gandhi. The prolonged Japanese efforts to capture Kohima and Imphal drained their resources, leading to the failure of Operation U-Go. Despite months of Japanese attacks, Commonwealth forces held their ground. They eventually counter-attacked, causing substantial losses to the Axis-led forces, forcing them to retreat into Burma.

6

Legacy

On 18th August 1945, at around 2.30 pm, in Taihoku (in Taiwan), Bose boarded a flight. However, the ill-fated flight took a grim turn as the plane veered from its standard take-off path, accompanied by a loud noise akin to engine backfiring. The portside engine and propeller fell from the aircraft, causing it to swing wildly and crash in flames, leading to the instant deaths of several passengers, including key personnel. Among these were the chief pilot, co-pilot, and Lieutenant-General Tsunamasa Shidei, the Vice Chief of Staff of the Japanese Kwantung Army and the designated negotiator for Bose's dealings with the Soviet army in Manchuria, lost their lives instantly.

Subash Chandra Bose getting on the ill-fated aircraft

Upon regaining consciousness, Habibur Rahman – who was Bose's assistant – and Bose made an attempt to escape through the rear door, only to discover it obstructed by luggage. In desperation, they opted to dash through the flames and make their exit from the front. Bose, soaked in gasoline, survived but suffered severe burns. As the ground staff approached the aircraft, they witnessed two individuals staggering towards them, with Bose resembling a human torch due to his ignited clothes. Rahman and members of the ground staff were able to smother the flames. However, they noticed that Bose's head and face were severely burnt.

Bose was rushed to the Nanmon Military Hospital in Taihoku. The airport staff contacted Dr. Taneyoshi Yoshimi, the head surgeon at the hospital, at approximately 3 pm. Upon arrival at the hospital, Bose remained conscious and reasonably coherent for some time. Dr. Yoshimi promptly observed severe third-degree burns on numerous areas of his body, particularly his chest, casting significant doubt on his chances of survival.

Despite the treatment, Bose slipped into a coma. Between 9 and 10 pm, on the fateful day, Subhas Chandra Bose breathed his last, aged 48. Two days later, his body was cremated in the main Taihoku crematorium. On 23rd August 1945, the Japanese news agency Do Trzei officially reported the passing of Bose and Shidei. Subsequently, on 7th September, a Japanese officer by the name of Lieutenant Tatsuo Hayashida transported Bose's cremated remains to Tokyo.

The following morning, these ashes were entrusted to Rama Murti, the president of the Tokyo Indian Independence League. Later, on 14th September, a memorial ceremony was conducted in Tokyo to honour Bose, and shortly thereafter, the ashes were consigned to the care of the priest at the Renkōji Temple, associated with Nichiren Buddhism in Tokyo. Since then, they have remained at this location.

Reactions

Among the INA personnel, many felt disbelief, shock, and trauma. The majority of those deeply affected were young Tamil Indians from Malaya and Singapore, both men and women, who made up the majority of civilian recruits in the INA.

Back in India, the official stance of the Indian National Congress was conveyed in a letter by Mahatma Gandhi to Rajkumari Amrit Kaur. Gandhi remarked, "Subhas Bose has died well. He was undoubtedly a patriot, though misguided." However, many Congress members had not forgiven Bose for his disagreements with Gandhi and for what they perceived as collaboration with Japanese fascism.

In addition, the Indian soldiers in the British Indian army, numbering around two and a half million, who had fought in World War II, had mixed feelings about the INA. Some viewed the INA as traitors and wanted them punished, while others were more sympathetic. Although the INA never posed a significant threat to the British Rule, the British government initially tried 300 INA officers for treason during the INA trials but later reversed course.

A significant number of Subhas Chandra Bose's followers, particularly in West Bengal, have consistently questioned both the fact and the details surrounding his death. This skepticism emerged immediately after his demise and has endured over time, giving rise to numerous conspiracy theories. These theories, which materialised shortly after his passing, continue to circulate, nurturing various myths and legends surrounding Bose's life and death.

A Timeless Influence

Subhas Chandra Bose has been honoured in various ways across India. His image appeared on Indian postage stamps in 1964, 1993, 1997, 2001, 2016, 2018, and 2021. Additionally, he was commemorated on ₹2 coins in 1996 and 1997, a ₹75 coin in 2018, and a ₹125 coin in 2021. Many significant places and institutions in India bear his name, including the Netaji Subhas Chandra Bose International Airport in Kolkata, Netaji Subhash Chandra Bose Island (formerly Ross Island), Netaji Subhash Chandra Bose Junction Gomoh Railway Station, and the Netaji Express, a train that operates between Howrah and Kalka.

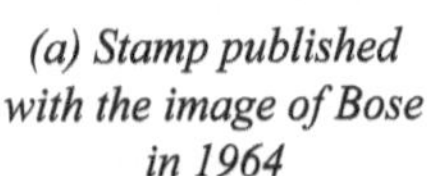

(a) Stamp published with the image of Bose in 1964

(b) Coin issued by RBI on the 100th Birth Anniversary of Subhas Chandra Bose

(c) Postal Stamp launched by the Indian Government in 2018 to mark 75th Anniversary of flag hoisting in Port Blair

Notably, on 23rd August 2007, late Japanese Prime Minister Shinzō Abe paid a visit to Netaji Bhawan in Kolkata. During his visit, he expressed deep admiration for Bose's leadership in the Indian independence movement against British rule and conveyed the Japanese people's profound respect for Netaji. In recognition of his contributions, Shinzō Abe was awarded the Netaji Award in 2022.

In a significant development in 2021, the Government of India declared 23rd January as Parakram Divas, commemorating Bose's birth anniversary. However, the Trinamool Congress (TMC) and the All India Forward Bloc advocated for observing the day as Deshprem Divas. To mark his 125th birth anniversary, a holographic statue of Bose was installed at India Gate; it was later replaced by a permanent granite statue. These commemorations underscore the lasting impact of Netaji Subhas Chandra Bose on India's history and collective memory.

7

Philosophy and Ideology

The life and legacy of Subhas Chandra Bose are characterised by a profound philosophical and ideological underpinning that transcended his time and left a mark on India's struggle for independence. Bose was a visionary leader who charted an unconventional path in the pursuit of India's liberation from Colonial rule. His devotion to the cause of independence was deeply rooted in his philosophical outlook, which emphasised the primacy of action and sacrifice. Bose believed that freedom was not merely a political objective but a moral imperative, and he was willing to go to great lengths to achieve it.

Central to Bose's philosophy was the rejection of passive resistance and non-violence as the sole means of attaining freedom. He advocated for a more assertive and militant approach, believing that India could only secure its independence through resolute action. This philosophy culminated in the formation of the INA, a testament to his belief in the power of armed struggle against colonial oppression.

Furthermore, Bose's ideology extended beyond India's borders, forging international alliances to garner support for the cause. His interactions with international political leaders demonstrated his pragmatic approach to achieving India's freedom, even if it meant engaging with ideological adversaries.

Spirituality

Subhas Chandra Bose drew profound inspiration from the *Bhagavad Gita* in his fight against British rule. From an early age, he was deeply influenced by Swami Vivekananda's universalist teachings, nationalist ideas, and emphasis on social reform. These interpretations of India's ancient scriptures resonated with him, and Hindu spirituality played a significant role in his political and social beliefs.

Throughout his life, Bose's philosophy and ideological outlook were deeply rooted in his spiritual and nationalist convictions, which guided his relentless pursuit of India's independence from British colonial rule.

Authoritarianism

Bose believed that adopting authoritarian methods could lead to India's liberation and societal reconstruction. He admired the authoritarian regimes in Italy and Germany during the 1930s and saw potential in applying similar approaches to achieve Indian independence.

While Bose's program shared some similarities with Japanese fascists, this led to his marginalisation within the Congress party. Consequently, he sought alliances with fascist regimes to oppose British rule and eventually left India. Bose argued that India needed an authoritarian political system with a strong central government and dictatorial powers for a certain period of time.

Legend of Gumnami Baba
Netaji's death remains a mystery. After the widely discussed plane crash in Taiwan on 18th August 1945, it was believed that Bose assumed the identity of a *sadhu* and lived in Uttar Pradesh, known to people as Gumnami Baba. But this claim hasn't been substantiated.

Initially, Bose had faith in democracy as the best choice for India. However, during the early 1930's, Bose began to doubt whether a democratic system could effectively address India's poverty and social inequalities. He believed that a socialist state akin to Soviet Russia, which he admired, was necessary for national reconstruction.

Bose's wartime alliance with the Axis powers was driven by a combination of pragmatism and a deep commitment to Indian nationalism. He was not a Nazi or a Fascist, as he supported women's empowerment, secularism, and other liberal ideas. Some argue that Bose's approach was rooted in his nationalist fervour, while others see it as a strategic mobilisation tactic common among post-colonial leaders.

8

Notable Achievements

In the annals of India's struggle for independence, the name Subhas Chandra Bose will always hold a special place. His life and achievements are a testament to an unshakeable resolve, relentless dedication, and an indomitable spirit that continues to inspire generations of Indians.

Netaji Subhas Chandra Bose, often addressed as "Netaji" with deep reverence, emerged as one of the most charismatic and influential leaders during India's quest for freedom. His devotion to the cause of liberating India from British colonial rule led him on a tumultuous journey filled with daring escapades and audacious plans.

A towering figure in the fight against British oppression, Bose left an enduring legacy on the pages of Indian history. He continues to serve as a beacon of hope and determination for all those who yearn for freedom and justice. Let us delve into the remarkable achievements of this great leader:

1. One of Bose's most iconic achievements was the formation of the INA in 1942. This army of Indian soldiers, along with Japanese support, aimed to liberate India from British rule. Bose's leadership inspired thousands of Indians to join the INA, marking a significant challenge to British rule.

2. Bose served as a youth educator and commandant of the Bengal Congress volunteers.

3. Bose encountered multiple incarcerations during his active involvement in the independence movement. Following his release from prison in 1927, he took a significant step by launching a newspaper named *Swaraj*.

4. Before his international feats, Bose was a prominent leader within the Indian National Congress. He was elected as the Congress President in 1938 and 1939, advocating for a more aggressive approach toward attaining independence.

5. In 1938, Bose assumed the presidency of the Indian National Congress. During his tenure, he established a planning committee responsible for devising an industrialisation policy for the country.

6. Bose championed the cause of social equality and opposed caste-based discrimination within the Indian National Congress. His advocacy for marginalised communities and inclusivity left a lasting impact on the freedom movement.

7. In 1939, the All India Forward Bloc, a left-wing nationalist party led by Bose, merged with the Indian National Congress. This move was aimed at uniting the party's radical members within the Forward Bloc faction.

8. He travelled extensively during World War II, seeking international support for India's cause. He forged alliances with nations like Nazi Germany, Imperial Japan, and Fascist Italy, demonstrating his diplomatic skills and his resolve to leveraging any available means to further India's struggle for independence.

9. Bose established the Provisional Government of Free India (Azad Hind Government) in Singapore in 1943. It was recognised by several Axis powers, and Bose served as the head of this government. This move symbolised the assertion of India's sovereignty and government-in-exile.

10. Bose's Azad Hind Radio broadcasted proclamations, speeches, and news updates to rally support for India's independence struggle. Phrases like *"Jai Hind"* and "Give me blood, and I shall give you freedom" became iconic slogans associated with his broadcasts.

11. He raised the Indian Flag on the Andaman Islands, which were under Japanese occupation at the time.

12. Bose authored several books, including his autobiography *An Indian Pilgrim* and *The Indian Struggle*, which chronicles the independence movement. These works continue to provide insights into the era's history.

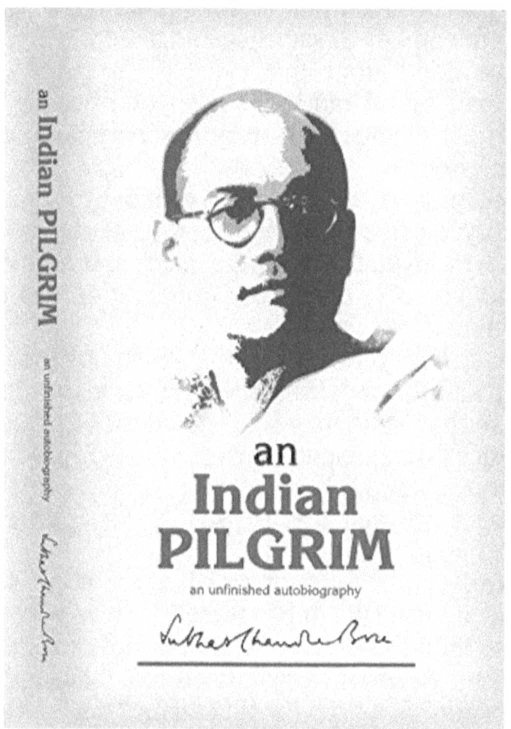

Cover of the unfinished biography of Subhas Chandra Bose -An Indian Pilgrim

❑❑❑

9

Subhas Chandra Bose's Famous Quotes

Here are a few inspiring quotes by Netaji Subhas Chandra Bose that reflect his fervent commitment to India's independence and his belief in the power of sacrifice and action:

- "It is blood alone that can pay the price of freedom. Give me blood and I will give you freedom."
- "No real change in history has ever been achieved by discussions."
- "Men, money, and materials cannot by themselves bring victory or freedom. We must have the motive-power that will inspire us to brave deeds and heroic exploits."
- "Undoubtedly, purity and moderation are essential in childhood and youth."
- "Never lose your faith in the destiny of India."
- "We should have but one desire today - the desire to die so that India may live - the desire to face a martyr's death, so that the path to freedom may be paved with the martyr's blood."
- "Forget not that the grossest crime is to compromise with injustice and wrong."
- "Life loses half its interest if there is no struggle – if there are no risks to be taken."
- "One individual may die for an idea, but that idea will, after his death, incarnate itself in a thousand lives."
- "Freedom is not given, it is taken."
- "Soldiers who always remain faithful to their nation, who are always prepared to sacrifice their lives, are invincible."
- "A true soldier needs both military and spiritual training."
- "Reality is, after all, too big for our frail understanding to fully comprehend. Nevertheless, we have to build our life on the theory which contains the maximum truth."

10

Learning from Bose's Life

Subhas Chandra Bose's life is a source of enduring inspiration, offering a wealth of lessons that continue to guide and motivate us. His remarkable journey towards India's independence and his commitment to justice provide profound insights that can shape our own lives and actions.

One of the most striking aspects of Bose's character was his unwavering determination and perseverance. Throughout his life, he demonstrated that a strong resolve is essential for achieving even the loftiest of goals. His resilience in the face of numerous challenges and obstacles serves as a powerful reminder that persistence is often the key to realising our dreams.

Bose's life was marked by extraordinary courage. Whether it was defying the British authorities, seeking support from unlikely sources, or leading the Indian National Army (INA), he exemplified the importance of courage in confronting injustice. His actions remind us that courage is a fundamental quality for effecting change.

As a leader, Subhas Chandra Bose exhibited exceptional vision and the ability to mobilise people. His leadership skills were instrumental in uniting diverse groups and individuals for the common goal of a free and united India. His vision serves as a testament to the impact of visionary leadership.

Bose's international outreach and diplomacy are also instructive. He sought assistance from various nations, even those with conflicting interests, emphasising the importance of international cooperation in achieving common objectives. His approach inspires us to transcend differences and collaborate for the greater good.

Moreover, inclusivity was a hallmark of Bose's approach to the freedom struggle. He believed in uniting people from diverse backgrounds and ideologies for a shared purpose. This inclusive ethos underscores the value of unity in the pursuit of collective goals.

Subhas Chandra Bose's willingness to make personal sacrifices for the greater good is a powerful lesson. His famous words, "Give me blood, and I shall give you freedom," remind us of the selflessness required for meaningful change. His commitment to a cause larger than himself inspires acts of sacrifice for the greater good.

The enduring legacy of independence that Subhas Chandra Bose left behind serves as a constant reminder that freedom is non-negotiable. His life story encourages us to stand up against oppression and injustice, knowing that the fight for liberty is worth every sacrifice.

Perhaps the most enduring lesson from Bose's life is the principle of never giving up. His commitment to the idea of freeing India from colonial rule serves as a beacon of hope for anyone facing seemingly insurmountable challenges. In Bose's determination, we find a timeless source of inspiration to persist in the face of adversity and work tirelessly toward our convictions.

Subhas Chandra Bose's life imparts invaluable lessons: determination, courage, visionary leadership, international cooperation, inclusivity, selflessness, respect for diversity, the legacy of independence, and an attitude of never giving up. These lessons, when applied to our own lives, can empower us to create a better, more just world, just as Netaji did in his relentless pursuit of India's freedom.